Selected Poems

by
MIODRAG PAVLOVIĆ

Translated by

JAMES SUTHERLAND-SMITH
and NENAD ALEKSIĆ

CROMER

PUBLISHED BY SALT
12 Norwich Road, Cromer, Norfolk NR27 0AX
All rights reserved

© Miodrag Pavlović, 2014
Tranlsations © James Sutherland-Smith and Nenad Aleksić

The right of Miodrag Pavlović to be identified as the
author of this work has been asserted by him in accordance
with Section 77 of the Copyright, Designs and Patents Act 1988.

This book is in copyright. Subject to statutory exception
and to provisions of relevant collective licensing agreements,
no reproduction of any part may take place without the written
permission of Salt Publishing.

Salt Publishing 2014

Printed and bound in the United Kingdom by Lightning Source UK Ltd

Typeset in Paperback 9 / 13

*This book is sold subject to the conditions that it shall not,
by way of trade or otherwise, be lent, re-sold, hired out,
or otherwise circulated without the publisher's prior consent
in any form of binding or cover other than that in which
it is published and without a similar condition including this
condition being imposed on the subsequent purchaser.*

ISBN 978 1 84471 959 4 paperback

1 3 5 7 9 8 6 4 2

Selected Poems

MIODRAG PAVLOVIĆ, 1928–2014, was one of the three great poets of modern Serbian poetry along with Vasko Popa and Ivan Lalić. In addition to being a poet he was an essay writer, playwright, literary critic novelist.

His poetry appeared on the Serbian literary scene after World War Two and marked a radical change in taste and poetic expression both breaking with avant-garde and surrealist poetry without embracing socialist realism. Pavlović's poetry at first combined realism with a classical aesthetic to express the horror felt in the decades after the war and later used material from on myths, custom and history in Serbian culture.

Pavlović was Director of the Belgrade National Theatre Drama and in 1961 he started working as an editor for the publishing house Prosveta in Belgrade and held the position for twenty years.

Pavlović received a great number of important awards and prizes for his literary work within the former Yugoslavia and in 2003 the City of Münster European Prize for poetry. He was nominated twice for the Nobel Prize for Literature. In 1970 he became the fifth Golden Wreath Laureate of the Poetry Evenings at Struga, an honour subsequently given to Auden, Neruda, Montale, Alberti, Enzensberger, Ritsos, Ginsberg, Rozewicz, Hughes, Brodsky, Bonnefoy, Heaney, Darwish and Transtromer among others. His work has also been translated into Polish, German, French, Macedonian, Rumanian, Slovak, Greek, Hungarian, Bulgarian and Swedish. This selection is the first in English is the first since 1989.

Contents

Introduction: Miodrag Pavlović	xi
'What have you lost'	1
'This woman, unknown to me'	3
Death of the Lovers	5
Madrigals for Her	6
from Defending Our City	8
Lokrum	9
Calypso and Odysseus	10
Odysseus on Circe's Island	12
Itea	13
Spellbound Fetters	15
The Rhine Valley	16
Amiens	18
Chartres	20
La Rotonda	22
A Visit to St. Trophime D'arles	24
Descent to Limbo	26
from Metamorphoses	28
Bread and Wine	30
The Dragon Slayer	32
from Singing at the Whirlpool	33
from Links	55
from The Moon's Wedding	63
from Sequence	69
from Second Sequence	100
from Third Sequence	104
from The Wise and Foolish Virgins	107
The Lovers in the Church	110
Bacchus and Ariadne in Naxos	111
Entering Cremona I	112
Giorgione: La Tempesta	113

Visiting the Zoological Gardens in Winter	114
Emmanuel De Witt: A Girl at the Virginals	117
A Flemish Painter	118
Imaginary Journey	120
from The Danube Valley	122
from Orgia Sacra	123
The End of the Orgy	124
from The Science of the Soul	126
Note	129

Introduction
Miodrag Pavlović

Miodrag Pavlović was born in 1928 in Novi Sad the second city of Serbia and the chief city of the Vojvodina region which extends north to the border with Hungary and west to the border with Croatia. It is a Danube port city situated between the old territory of the Austro-Hungarian Empire and that part of Serbia which was in the Ottoman Empire for five hundred years. Pavlović, like the city of his birth, contains not only the ancient cultures of Serbia, but also a generous element of the cultures of Europe. In addition to Serbian he was fluent in English, French and German. He trained and practiced for a while in Belgrade as a doctor of medicine before choosing to pursue his calling in literature, having in 1952 already published his first collection, *87 Poems*, a book which can be said to have inaugurated modernism in Serbian literature. He worked as a literary editor and also wrote short stories, novels and a number of important works in literary criticism. From his withdrawal from active work as a publisher he divided his time between his homes in Tuttingen in Germany and in Belgrade. Miodrag Pavlović was an extremely prolific poet, but only a tiny fraction of his work has made its way into English in book and chapbook form. Like many Serbian writers his fluency in a number of languages meant that he was also a distinguished translator and he mentioned to me when we first met that he had even translated Sir Geoffrey Hill's work. He was a regular nominee for the Nobel Prize in literature.

The selection consists mostly of poems previously untranslated or at least uncollected in English. I suggested that new translations one or two of his more celebrated poems might be a good idea, but was told in no uncertain terms by the poet that he wished for other poems to be translated. Moreover, he wished for the selection to come from the first volume of his Collected Poems, published in 2000 by the publishing house Prosveta, called *Iskon* or Origins. I use the word translated from the French of the late Robert Marteau's essay at the end of Barry Callaghan's Pavlović translations, *A Voice Locked in Stone* (Exile editions, 1985), as opposed to 'Yore' used by Bernard Johnson in his translations *The Slavs Beneath Parnassus* (Angel Books 1985). Yore is an archaic expression which seems hopelessly inappropriate.

The other two volumes are respectively *Izbor* (*Choice*) and *Ischod* (*Consequence*). Pavlović organised the volumes so that although they follow a chronology the first two volumes overlap and the 1963 collection, *Mleko Iskoni* (*Milk of Origins*) has a selection in both the first two volumes and it seems that Pavlović organised his collected poems into three distinct thematic areas. In the note at the end of Origins Pavlović declared that the poems were chosen from 1946 to 1996 on the basis of their similarity, 'the concreteness of sensory perceptions, erotic inspiration and nature.' The selection in Choice was from historical inspiration particularly from Hellenic and Slavic history together with poems from childhood and the war and other 'cataclysms.' Consequence has prose poems from Pavlović's last period of a philosophical and religious nature.

However, the three volumes are not thematically exclusive and historical and religious motifs are apparent in Origins. 87 Poems may be regarded as an historic breakthrough in Slovak modernism, but Pavlović gave his first collection short thrift in his Collected Poems with only twelve surviving. We have translated six of these and they are very much poems of a brilliant debut. In the 1930s and after the Second World War the Surrealist poets dominated the avant-garde. They were left-leaning and were well connected with the post-war Communist establishment. Consequently, unlike their counterparts further north there was not a rush by former surrealists to turn out dutiful, conventional civic verse to establish their credentials with regimes that required socialist realism in the arts. Poets in the then Yugoslavia retained some freedom of expression and on the eve of Tito's formal break with the Soviet Union Pavlović was able to publish work which was sensual, violent and personal without reference to the building of socialism and could declare

> In your lap I've found more paradise
> Than can be hoped for at the end of life.
> (Madrigals for her)

Pavlović was not immune from patriotism in his poetry. So in *Defending Our City* his elegy sets out as 'one more lament at the attempt at solitude' which is subsumed by the destruction of Belgrade so that he must

> let our love declare it is part
> of a grief that is pride once more

In the second stanza Belgrade becomes personified in a manner familiar in the poems of Pablo Neruda replacing the lover in the first stanza and addressed with complex feelings of pride:

> My city, you were a widow and your sons unwidowed you,
> you remained on the tower with your husbands,
> in our rooms pride in the laments,
> the sunlit ridge of our gaze.

In the collection *Octaves* (1957) the sensuality has become knowing and disillusion has set as in Lokrum:

> Adventure revealed is an innate swindle of all manner and form.
> Now we think how lovely it is outside the garden, on the other side of the wall.

This weariness is pursued in *Milk of Origins* (1963) in the poems derived from Hellenic themes with Odysseus on Circe's island assuming an allegorical significance:

> We are bewildered pigs
> Under whom there is an irresolute ship.

In the companion poem it is evident that Pavlović had become a master of developing a theme in this the attraction and ultimate incompatibility of masculine and feminine with its thrilling last two lines:

> Oh, love, devastating for a man!
> And for a goddess too burdensome!

This technical mastery produced poems set in France, Germany and Italy, fantasias of relationships set in what seems to be a latter day grand tour. These are succeeded by a group of poems in *Light and Dark Holy Days* (1971) which contain a number of lyrical masterpieces such as *Bread and Wine*, perhaps with Holderlin's great poem in the background, the famous *Dragon Slayer*, culminating in extremely complex poems such as *Descent to Limbo* and *Metamorphoses* of which we have translated only the first part. Here Pavlović seems to call into question his mastery of language:

> First, the word-cancers
> and the words that taste like gunpowder

After 1971 Pavlović seems to have turned away from the complex stanza and the sensuous snares of complex metaphor. In a number of cycles, *Singing at the Whirlpool*, *Links*, and three *Sequences* he has shortened his line and almost eliminated punctuation. The first two of these take their inspiration from Neolithic sites by the Danube and conjure up a Dream Time akin to that of native Australians where the natural world and human consciousness are mingled in a perpetual present and the living co-exist with *The Dead*:

> They love to joke
> to trip you up
> push you in the river
> screech near an owl
> while we're asleep
> the dead fuss over themselves
> bone idle
> they live

> on our compassion
> now and then heal somebody
> when they meet
> they dream
> that they're all alone in the world

In the second sequence recent history arrives, as in *Belgrade 1941* where

> With a torch between his legs
> a scoundrel flies
> and burns houses
>   skins
>   graves

and in the third poems located in the natural world are interspersed with references to Christianity although Pavlović's theology seems to approach the bleak territory of Thomas Hardy's view of divinity:

> A spirit, that copes with lawlessness
> barely, and a son, in a world without mercy
> dedicated to love, to which nothing compares
> in weight, in dimension.

In the collection *Entering Cremona* (1989) Pavlović recovered his earlier eloquence in a series of poems with other arts as a point of departure. *Giorgione: La Tempesta* has a bitter authority:

> Separation begins when maturity passes.
> Everybody stands on his own side of the river.
> The town is not just closed, it exists less.
> Exile is more necessary than courage.

A Flemish Painter, which Pavlović told me is a 'key poem', is at first reading a monologue where the painter decides to paint still lifes, but in expressing a contempt for history, 'even ragmuffins / look refined / when they're eating melon', reveals that pure painting becomes impure, 'Oh misery, / this pot of beer / costs/ as if it were gold.'

There is much more in this selection from the first volume of Pavlović's Collected Poems than simply 'the concreteness of sensory perceptions, erotic inspiration and nature.' The energy and sensuality of the early poetry gave way to eloquence and was succeeded by what was described in Spanish modernism as a *depuración* in language and form enabling Pavlović to bring together prehistory and contemporary civilisation in a poetry which has few equals in range of form and richness of language. He is regarded as one of the three great names in late twentieth century poet alongside Vasko Popa (1922–1991) and Ivan Lalić (1931–1996). Popa was made famous to English readers through the Penguin Modern European Poets series and the slightly mythomaniac advocacy of Ted Hughes. Lalić was famously translated by Francis Jones. Consequently, although Pavlović has been translated by distinguished small presses in Britain and Northern America he never received the exposure his two compatriots received outside a coterie readership of poetry in the English-speaking world. This selection hopes to begin to redress the balance with this selection from Origins. The translations were the joint work of Nenad Aleksić and myself with an editing session with Miodrag in the conference room at the British Council in Belgrade. Despite his age he went through our draft in great detail pointing out inaccuracies and sometimes demanding from me 'a better word choice, please James.' It was a humbling yet inspiring experience.

While this selection was in proof Miodrag Pavlović died on 17 August 2014 in Tuttlingen in Germany.

JAMES SUTHERLAND-SMITH
Prešov, Slovakia

Selected Poems

'What have you lost'

What have you lost
in this forest
where the wind
hoists its flags?

Neither hand nor gold
nor a filament of your wits

On to dry leaves
on to moist shadows
a confession
of flesh has fallen

A confession
of trampling upon cyclamen
has fetched the prisoner
back to the ship

While other people's feet
stamp at your temples
with a furious poem

Look at the stars
the only salvation is
a fortunate insensibility
What have you lost

When has flesh
confessed?
Oh slave
Sleep
The night is short!

'This woman, unknown to me'

This woman, unknown to me
sits in my room
hiding her face

I enter
and find my hands
in her hair

Nakedness
is the creation
of my thumb

A women is
created
by nakedness

Warm roads
across silk underwear
lead to a boat

There is moonlight on the hill
and the wind blows
through black thickets

A yellow rib
has fallen on to the plate
among grapes

Two swords have stuck a tree
tendons cracked
and fire flared

The roots of the embers
grow in young innards
sucking blood

Hands in the dark
tremble
like cries in a storm

Beneath a sweaty chest
closed eyes slip

The blind
are before the smashed gates

On to the dry earth
hot drops fall
beyond the neck of a bird
butchered by feet

Death of the Lovers

Head to head in the pale palm of a hand they lie;
On a dark star loving one another a man, a woman
And while their hair floats over limbs and loins
Clods of blood calve heavily and more heavily.

In the gloom what comes close vanishes from sight
And when the black hills oscillate space
On a naked back a big hard fish presses
Its lips and the love of the eye goes out like a light.

In the field where the wind slashes the dry grass
A deaf pit opens in the earth until dawn
And in folds of light the necessary trees grow.

Seeing in the serene head's undisturbed embrace
When to preserve the dead the owl glides in,
The swallows unravel tangles of hair

Madrigals for Her

1.

Come and bring
Honey in a glass
And the secret seed.

Go and take
A joyful doom
And time redeemed.

When the overripe bone kneels down;
A bridge stands between the grave and the sun.

2.

When we meet again
You will see the sight of a face after the rain
And lips wounded by solitude.

When we meet again
You will get a great strawberry that breathes
And love that thickens from waiting.

But now sit calm and pale,
While the moon splits, fidelity stays whole.

3.

Completely alone are the two of us
Barefoot we tiptoe on the sonorous terraces
And no-one has a clue where we might go

We become one in maternal darkness
A double brow gleams white above a kiss
And eternal embraces from the belly grow.

In your lap I've found more paradise
Than can be hoped for at the end of life.

6.

You have to love at a hidden table
That is covered by the smell of skin
Awakened at the window of the will.

You have to come to terms with the pain
If the clash of the disappointed spectres can
Transform a brow into undying vigils.

But let young fingers freely make
New forms in mud and muck.

from *Defending Our City*

iv

Once more un-alone in our room,
I shall utter a reminiscent lament to you,
the two of us in our room,
one more lament in the attempt at solitude
in a room, above rooms that have been destabilized,
not by superstructure but by a cannonball,
above walls that tilted before dying,
above graves impaled on a stake,
above the irrecoverable heat of the bed,
once more on graves suspended upon a lamp-post,
on death in a ravine of the earth and sky,
on the five centuries of ravens on tables,
let our love declare it is part
of a grief that is pride once more.

Oh my city, tower of husbands,
Sky-parched forest, in a ravine of fires,
you were a widow,
they attacked you with the tooth and hair of lust,
they set you on fire and those who did burned themselves,
they starved you and died of hunger themselves,
they plundered you and fell into a pit of centuries,
they strangled you and choked themselves in the storm,
you choked the storms.
My city, you were a widow and your sons unwidowed you,
you remained on the tower with your husbands,
in our rooms pride in the laments,
the sunlit ridge of our gaze.

Lokrum

We are imprisoned by the sea, and it is only where the flowerbeds begin
That we've been looking for in our long stroll in the dusk
We, a nameless multitude dressed in loving skin.
We disrobe before the beginning of beauty at the edge of death
And permit our limbs to sink towards a sumptuous garden,
We are bathers that bicker over the last piece of the sun.
In couples we step over the bones of the bloody shapes of our ancestors
Turned black-and-blue from a deadlock of thoughts and the hand of a
    barren creator.

And such a stroll it is! We hover above a trencher board of corals
And we listen to the birds on an umbilical cord like a tree
Eternal as the wave etched into the crystal force of the eye.
It's water no longer; in our fingers there's a resistance of cymbals
Pressed against us as if they wish to wrestle;
Everything chimes, music gushes out from the stony flow
And overwhelms us, the blade has already slid aloud into tissue.
We are now at the hearth of things from which a living thought issues.

And then love stops since the aromas of grasses
Surpass all that a state of passion proffers,
And where we have managed to sketch our bodies with precision
We do not care for the touch: in the heart of reality we are drowsy.
Here in the garden of paradise we devise ways to save ourselves from
    salvation; contagious
Boredom and another face diminish through the gate, the whole
Adventure revealed is an innate swindle of all manner and form.
Now we think how lovely it is outside the garden, on the other side of
    the wall.

Calypso and Odysseus

Every night in the cave
She has clasped that man
Not for gold and fog
But for male flesh.
Into her eternal time
He roots himself like a mountain
Beneath which everything burns.
Yet, she has sensed under her hand
That his tissues are ageing
Like the sand rustling in an hourglass,
And she has heard in the midst of the love fury
The human bloodstream across from her
Whimpering so like a child
Shut in behind an underground door.

He has sombrely clasped the flesh of the women
Whom he cannot harm
Though she is humble, her limbs are lovely:
An exemplar of the dance, texture of the rays
On which the pillars of the temple hang!
Displayed to light day and night,
In her hands is his torso
Like the mire through which they wade,
From the divine pressure,
Nothing can save him,
He goes and plaits withies.

He is bored on the shore,
The boat is a conspiracy which cannot be trusted,
He is a forced member of a union with divinity.
He gazes at the searing main of the sea

And would like to cross over the water.
She is combing her hair in the dark of the cavern
And foresees his gasping breath.

For what is the embrace of two horizons
That wish reproach and sharp desire
for one another?
For the female god all is of worth
from the mortal world,
To be among goddesses
Is the greatest ascent for the husband.

And they both follow their own courses
Without a goodbye,
He goes home, knowing what awaits him beyond his gates,
She to a higher severity of concept
Excited by the contact with death.
Odysseus departs
As if he descends from a lighthouse.

In sleep their breath is brought close,
Around midnight they truly love one another
From a distance, from opposite sides,
And they will never meet again
Not even beyond the horizon.

Oh, love, devastating for a man!
And for a goddess too burdensome!

Odysseus on Circe's Island

Almost every day Circe wishes to
Turn somebody into a pig,
Different names are mentioned, listen:
The herd increases, you meet friends in the street
Grunting! They complain, initiate law-suits
And beat their head against the fence,
Oh what times!

My friends ask me: where is the ship?
And I'm not in a hurry to embark them
On to a deck rotten and transparent
And I say: endure,
We are not yet ripe for justice,
If we will leave this place, what then?

The Ocean needs to traverse a rugged path,
And to lure the shadows to black blood,
When it actually comes to the sacrifice
Nobody will know their kin!
And we have deserved our pig condition
Let's say it straight out
For our adoration for a slut-woman
And our desire for the dark features of power.

I do not know when we will depart from this era
Circe is out of spells, infertile, stupid,
And she is set on holding us fast on the island,
We are bewildered pigs
Under whom there is an irresolute ship.

Itea

Rest from Delphi in the bay of Itea.
By the path through the olive fields come down among
    women
Pegging out laundry and throwing silk
Across the water and where Lenten soup boils over
As if again from the foam a goddess
Is to be born.
Fall down to the earth after the sanctuary
And sprout, go among the olives
That on a wave stand, on a wave drying
From the heat, and becoming red,
And catch the butterflies while they beat their wings
And suck out their sweet brains
Then touch the shells on the branches
Chirping to the slime, young, one-eyed,
Eager for knowledge before they depart for school
O how they tremble!
Forget the humble shadow of the sanctuary!
And a step ahead everything swarms with women
Little and naked like spilled almonds
That you take in your palm and nibble.

Is everything woven of feminine thread?
As soon as you descend a little, the world is of sex.
Look at the mystery of that elemental hill:
Two breasts stand on a cliff,
Different: one of mother-of-pearl and fresh morning
Grabs you by the scruff of the neck and calls you to the
    opaque whirlpool.
And the other, maternally grey

Warmly touches your cheek
And sees the victim in you.
Both on the same body:
The stretched morsel of a girl,
And the pelvis of a mother like a circular lullaby,
A deep cloud hides their head
In which sacrifice is made
There your body is burning now.

In the bay of Itea rest from Delphi.

Spellbound Fetters

That secret greater than all
Behind the door just by the core
And so close that it smirches our honour
That body is the only thing truly given
Into your hands
Find yourself on the coastal side
With pain and sand and a beautiful composition
Violence begins.

And yet the wedding clatter was heard
And a shirt discarded with a team of horses
Limb bargains with limb
And fence with fence
Under the armpit an expensive roll-on
Who leads us
To the ruins at the cost of darkness
Your knees slide
Almost to my lips
And someone watches the visceral curse.

I carry your thighs and the jug
On the stairs
As if I know where
Which part of the body would make me fall asleep
In the foreign country beyond the stars
Where there is no healing-path
Neither in the wild track of the hunter
Nor in the imperial movement of miracles!

The Rhine Valley

By the sound everything is close, autumn,
Crops in a hubbub, and the river ripens,
The sky will fall, dark fruits,
Everything required to draw together;
Crop embraces crop,
Woman a man, in the middle of a clear scene
Like watching ourselves from the sky.

The transparent grains merge,
The joining is speech and the branches are love,
And the lance of St. George that rushes through the vineyards
In the body of a dragon as in an ancient boat
Opens a wound to give birth to a people already gone.
And not to forget the sound: children singing
Beside the wall of the monastery, in fear
Of their voice that is so vast.

It's summer, everybody loves each other terribly,
Like forty victims on ice
So naked and mad with pleasure,
And I wanted only you
After seeing the whole of mankind.
We walk on without shame
To a piano in the middle of a field,
You are laughing, the piano is bigger than the fields
And an eagle is playing on it
A tune which opens the hills
And an old red harvest wells up;
An open radiant grave,
A rebellion of many sunrays,

Somebody severe and gentle watches us,
Maybe spring, a wonderful woman, or a wounded god,
They will lead us where it is required,
Or tell us to remain below, close to the wine.

Amiens

Why not, tonight, too,
I will sleep with the queen.
I have come to her city,
Got off at her square and I admire her body
Larger then the size of dream;
I knew that in life
This fortune can happen to me.
I buy newspapers and light my cigarette,
Then I look for a hotel nearby.
I open the window and in the red skies see:
Her wings in her hair, bells hang everywhere,
And her body grows, a volcano of sweet ills.

Even though it were in front of the head,
Those golden hands have to touch!
To peer into her expression,
Even if I ascend with difficulty,
On the alien side of dreams.
All is smooth, she admits me
And puts her hand to the back of my head –
I say: we haven't dined yet,
And the food is good here,
But the blue Teutonic eye is silent
And the northern seas touch the bed.
In the dream I fall asleep again, she departs,
The hush doubles.

I wake who knows when, I see a radiant stone,
Morning, the empty street – mine, and I leave:
In the dream I became a beggar
And forgot my shoes in the hotel,
My eye cannot reach her beauty,
Barefoot, in high hope I go round her.

Chartres

I would like to lead you into the temple as well, daughter,
And the high priests to move towards us,
Contrite, deeply affected, in the shadow of the pillars,
And while the people watch you and intuit signs,
For a dove of light to appear over the crown of your head.

But this has already happened for all of us.
And now a man walks from temple to temple
Seeks those memories, and they change, too,
They lead their meetings and battles
Of which not much is known: you see,
The ancient kings are naïve as puppets,
The lambs fatten in the eternal dew,
The roses planted into timelessness,
Are all larger, lush to monstrosity.
Grass that nobody grazes,
Becomes red and hangs on the walls
Like the expensive garments of the cardinal-ogre,
Only has a god remained small in the altar
And they say: dry like an old silk cocoon.

Oh, the eternal dew in the glass!
And the desert river in the marble!
Skeletons dressed in blue
Conceal their joints, dying of living shame.
You look at the horseman, the procession of guards,
And the wind of transfiguration that points backwards.
Treasury of playthings! Winter charms,
And the discovery:
That you are not our daughter any more, but a woman,
(You always were a woman)

The bride's veil falls over your head
And the roses alter their scent, the abysses of night
 animate.
Then the warriors revive from a brutal passion:
The spears are poisonous, the wounds in the paintings
 ache, –
Only through a woman do you truly suffer,
And the cocoons within her awake with a germ that shines.

La Rotonda

You saw, they go mad in the borough
When two love each other overmuch, and you're so right:
While we wonder, we don't consider them much.
Sulphur stinks behind us. Sodom,
We flee to the hills. Lot is there
And his daughter, both enormous,
Shamelessly uncovered before heaven.
They take our place. And it's not bad for them, either.
I wonder who was the more sinful: the scorched town
Or he, who is not that old?

We go from country to country, from circle to circle,
And look for a house, once in a while we find a pillar
And the walls of beauty, so that our envy grows
Because for us the beautiful buildings are always on the outside;
We embrace secretly in the attics in our dreams.
Is one supposed to display love in the square?
No, only the truly sinful can do that
And mad old people and girls hard as stone.

Move, Lot, take that woman in your arms
And go back to Sodom, that town is always whole!
Let us the guiltless plant a pole and build a cupola
On the abandoned hill
Before Adam dies;
We are to slide down the mirrors
Into the darkness of our bare needs, into the naked night!
Don't move, woman! I don't know where the dawn comes from.

All I can see is the cleft of your breasts
In the air, and crossed spears:
The battle is around us, the borough enraged,
We have to get home before dawn.

A Visit to St. Trophime D'arles

A bull crosses the square, at noon,
two black horns – two clock hands,
Excuse me, I'm a newcomer,
        bread and blood are offered to me,
I am meek, tender flesh,
        parliament has sent me
along the way I look at old sarcophagi
and our God with a sheaf of wheat,
he who worries about the real rain.
                      Fine.

Girls knit a song,
    I am by the stone,
gentlemen approach me,
    horns intersect,
I passing through the shadow of bell,
some old longings inside me.
I am offered a pillar, a dog hewn from a rock,
the smile of a girl from a stone flower.
Do you like olives?
        I have changed horses many times,
The small of my back hurts and I bring greetings,
        Do you know what the Slavonic brothers are?
They depart embracing into the clearing,
        the stairs collapse,
The log cabin burns and a bloody pit opens
Like an inverted cupola . . .
Greetings from Vladislav, Ninoslav,
Rastislav and Gojko.
        Your mitre is beautiful
and your shepherd's crook.

      Stay with us!
Oh, if we only all knew the same news!
Where I am from the dead fight, children make love,
I have to go back, I kiss your dry hand,
And it is just for you to float above the earth
On that wonderful pillar,
      Oh, I like that stone of yours,
Guard the portal from the tremors of hell.
My thanks for the wine,
Come to us soon,
Song is our beautiful cry.
How will you find us?
      Go from dawn to dawn,
From first light to first light.
      Goodbye.
Goodbye until Judgment Day!

Descent to Limbo

Here are we and the empty space,
in the emptiness exactly where we are is unknown,
and the beasts try to fill up the space:
they become larger,
their skeletons grow,
long pelts drag over the lawn
and the wind shakes their flabby heads –
bags of skin that stoke the fires
of the last human buildings.

The monsters totter,
        their sort is unknown,
they are similar to oil as it spreads,
their huge tongues are over us like wet laundry
and over everything an ink of illiterate darkness.
We are astonished how our eyesight still works
and counsel that we should shelter under the ground;
it's not exactly war, but go and hide
among former scum
that now look cheerful and modest
in comparison with ... all comparisons have fallen
and everybody's eyes are awry.
Who knows where the gates are?
The divine sends its last message
Over the pitch-dark.
The message no longer gets through
not even like a knife to our heart, ouch!
But then in the bottom of the hall, behold,
a little door opens on to a mouse hole
and a little light and a little creature

wants to break through to us with all its might!
Let the tiniest saviour come,
that mouse in view –
our great hope!

from *Metamorphoses*

i

Of many small bellows,
is the paunch of the king made,
It shrinks on his death bed
wheezing like a siren which summons all highlanders
to come to town and plunder
as they used to in the good old days
when warriors were robbers
quicker than maggots in a carcass.

And in the veins of the earth a heart attack begins,
in the earthquake the treasury opens,
jewels fall from the roof
and the winter stores are opened in the midst of summer,
so trading begins all over
where all stand on their heads and lose.
First, the word-cancers
and the words that taste like gunpowder,
barbaric and those from the goldsmith
(the first from books, the next from the goat)
so one doesn't know in bed any more
on which side a man stand
calling for a boat to convey him
and where is the lake of the women truly,
in which of two bodies?

The priest flees in the midst of this agony.
Don't ask why, these are the ways of the mountain,
they tear up his vestments, why can't a naked man
serve in the church?

The crowd uses the rags to blindfold their eyes
and avoid the light,
or hide their darkness.
From the cracked bells someone else's playing breaks through
as though from the huge skull of Samson;
someone has to stamp out the vipers from the dark
that are off their heads after the death of the king.
Who is the weakest among us,
Who handles the light best,
Let him come.
We are waiting for him with music behind the gate.

Bread and Wine

Wine is the storm, the drill and the boom,
Bread the delicate camp,
Wine is the bell tower, colossal and bare,
the first sentence of the dissident, click,
bread is a rampart of the wretched,
dining table for blindworms
and a garland over the Dead Sea,
wine is a tongue on fire,
a golden shackle of dreams,
dribble that grumbles sweetly,
bread is a salutation of gleanings,
good spawn from the daily rivers,
wine – the solid silver of rage,
between the two cities a ghostly murmur,
you abduct it in the gorge like a bride,
bread disclosed as a shining head.

Then the two forces catch up with each other
and their veins fraternize
before you, in a glass, at midnight:
from a dark blue bannock a pearl rolls down,
and a flowery branch boasts over the blood.
within you thirst darts its tongue like a lizard,
you rise rebellious with love
and ask for drink and blossom,
reversal rings in your ears.
At the table horror.
Salt on the finger of the students,
at dawn when everything is revealed –

the guard sleeps. Who will say tomorrow
in which body the bread transforms,
to what company the wine invites us!

The Dragon Slayer

Every year from the hill
on a horse white as lily-of-the-valley
a dragonfly comes down bound in an iron breastplate
and rears before a silver veil that gazes at him in tears.
The scallop of his palm touches the harp
and the trembling lip of the daughter of the duke.
Then he approaches the worm
that is known to come from
some stinking corner of the universe
and that his strength is got from the union
of different deaths in a hundred-headed marvel.
So this villain is killed, then, by the radiant knight
with his beauty and spear
And a choir of girls begins to sing from the hill
in his honour.

With his head on the shoulder of dawn
he goes on his way modestly
and sits under the narrow shade of a cedar
Slaves and spiders seize him there
and tear his body into sheaves
taking his head with special care
into the workshop and torment.

Now go and understand the world
after seeing the source of his being:
he, beloved by the gods,
that cut off the head of the emperor-worm,
eaten away by formic acid.

from *Singing at the Whirlpool*

HEAD

Our head
resembles the sun
sea shells
a scout fish
it is oval
        eloquent
hard as stone
when it sleeps
it goes out hunting
for the dead will address fire
or establish order from the village high points

When it thinks deeply
the head
itself
is the greatest treasure

SHIFTING THE RIVER

I saw a great big foot
how it impels the river
uphill and downhill
somebody lies
up in a gorge
and impels the river as he likes
I saw a chance here
and my foot hurts
I barely move
before I die
instead of a foot
I'll seize running water

Insects

Evening
is a mosquito
night is the eagle owl
morning opens
the wasp's nest
midday ardently woos
the bumblebee
the whole day is
under the sign of the bee
which works with a tongue that flowers
a man apart from this
weaves something

he and the spider

Wedding

She comes
fleet of foot
round
accustomed to fire
she comes to listen
to call children
to cherish us and the flame

you will give her
a skeleton as a gift
and yourself like a god

Appeal

Come the day after tomorrow
out of spite
come very close
large
      fattened up
                    docile
stop at the entrance
   at the gates
lower yourself on to our stone
and don't go away
until I've eaten
your thigh
              back
                          and a piece of neck

Beginning Of The Rite

Stone by stone
rock by rock
here are the doors
for the sun
there the road
to an underground breast

for the shrine
we clear a space
all around
we stand wherever
everyone ready to flinch
before the holy

and yet brother hates brother

Two Roads

One is a good road
and lit
much travelled
by wild animals
a tree
crags like eaves

On the other road
through a thicket
something snarls
a foul odour
withered leaf
and thorns

Along this road
which others shun
you set out out to see
what this evil is

Body and Soul

stone
seeds itself
from behind
with the help of its shadow

Root Cellar

In the salt shadow
here where food is preserved
the goddess has descended
deep beneath the vault
and does not wish to rise from the dark
they call her
come into the light of day
you are beautiful
everyone loves you
longing to make merry
at your betrothal

She does not emerge
her hand delivers food
in winter
                    across the threshold
she demands that the bearded blind man
serve her
and sing
about the birth of the temple

Recollection

It's said
that things used to be better
there was law and order
there was food for everyone
winter and summer
the sea was around us
we lived in it
settled and satiated
now we tug
at one of its sleeves
so it won't slip away

Words

As soon as it gets light
I'll tell them two new words
which came to me in a dream
like loot
they'll be speechless when they hear
what is *ßetween*
and when off my tongue rolls
ácross

Those studying *ßetween*
will tumble into a gorge
between two crags
those trusting in *ácross*
will not return
either by water
or the river bed

the young ask me
how words are forged

Shadow

The shadow
leads us through ravines
the shadow
competes with a whirlpool
in widow's weeds
to my own shadow
I have fed milk
given her
the blood of birds
with my lips
and across my body
she turned blue
and secretly
began to shine
then up above
all were moved to frown
and I returned my shadow
to my soul

Threat

Three birds
black
fly at me
they haven't closed in yet
I tell them to stop
to wheel in a circle
three black birds
fly at me
I talk fast
three black birds
through my body
migrate south

The Dead

They love to joke
to trip you up
push you in the river
screech near an owl
while we're asleep
the dead fuss over themselves
bone idle
they live
on our compassion
now and then heal somebody
when they meet
they dream
that they're all alone in the world

Idol

I don't know
who left the little man
on the road
why he was dropped
between two fields
by somebody's hand
he casts a spell
or utters something
to the people in the valley

I carry him
he walks all over me
I assume he knows where to

Apparition

An unknown person
in a boat
passes b y me
and asks for a little food
we give fruit
a piece of venison
and he eats fast
steers between the rocks
and vanishes

Thus it was last year, too

Reporting

There's been no news
since the death
of my grandfather
he couldn't recall either
the last time
news had come
or whether there'd be
news again
who'd be required to bring it
from wherever
and where would this news
come to rest?

Knowledge

Everything is true
as it seems
day and night
and in what happens
in dreams
the supreme will
and what is spoken
by a fish for the table
and a woman
who is clad in scales
they all say
the same

nobody imagines

Rosary

A little house
a tiny woman
wizened fish
a huge stone
a boatless river
a lingering murmur
in the distance
what is up there
and round here
and ahead

A great secret
and a scanty feast

A Stone Which Thinks

Creases on a stone
emerge
from within
a blood tide
our round pebble dreams
and sees
a dream
on the surface above
there is a brain

and on the brain a stone
hears everything
and floats

Deluge

In fact
all is flood
the world is falsely dry
we founder
a hill appears
above everything a drum is beaten
no one ditch
can divide
this stretch of water
blessed is the one
born in water
and who to the deluge remains
deaf

Prediction

Thus it will come to pass and we
big-heads
will remain as rocks
and invite those
who fear us
to hug and kiss us

there'll be feasting
when the spirits come from the forest
fish from the river
from the people
a single child

from *Links*

The Neolithic Here

Here around the Danube
There's still barley
Further north
The grasses are hollow
everything that man knows
achieved
     on a terrace
Is born from mire
     harvest and jugs
fly over the undergrowth
     wonderful birds
people hail each other
from the coast to the swamp
love the digs more and more

and discover skulls

Neolithic II

There are more of us
track goes across track
tribes multiply
you meet a smiling face
near the water
      on the tree
between two shacks
and near the herd

the same behind the hill

they laugh the most
when looking down
on those who climb
      the cliffs

Dining Room

A great hall
along table
under the dome
a babble
people wait to eat
then plates land
everyone receives
a portion of their satiety
from the gallery
a cook in white watches
Are the people about to
perform something
otherwise
why are they eating?

A Former Faith

They found a church
from ancient times
full of salamanders
after the rain
on the floor
      amongst the gravel
the priest of the unknown religion
sits and writes

When they asked him
what else he remembers
he said
      nothing else

Old Ritual

Everything closed
as used to be around the city
now they will sacrifice women
white
to a new god
similar to the big antennae
haters dressed in robes
sharpening their keys
and moving towards the bodies
naked under the smoke

Later they will mourn for them
and pray

New Ritual

Once funerals
were normal
now you just see
black processions going
round the low-rise houses
go into the shops
and ask about the neighbourhood
something stings you
when they submit an account
to pay for the funeral
and they don't even have a dead body

Belgrade 1941

With a torch between his legs
a scoundrel flies
and burns houses
                    skins
                            graves
books become a bubble
birds wonder
are they cold
to have started so many fires
the town gains its ruins
the trees clutch their heads
who dares to take
apocalypse
into his hands

xxx

They steal everything
bulbs mail
milk
and empty bags
if at least they were cheerful
the neighbours
but they don't even give you
the time of day
they scratch the walls
plant trash
from their eyes
a dark mixture leaks
the only bright spot
the antennae on the roof
below are thieves
with big ears

from *The Moon's Wedding*

4.

The duke sees the peacock and the women
the apparition of the earth that he ploughs
lasts longest
and then he who sits at the head of the table
and keeps summoning by hand
offers power and easily-won honour
and the other
Stephen's deacon and village chief
       withdrew into himself
to withstand the experience
of a layer
after which you can only write satire
and sees apparitions of a gathering
above the stone field
gross bodies memory of the holy
who with their elbows leaning on the mountain
       and naked
wait for those that are called
to come to begin again
and in the creation of a new world.
use different materials.

That the archangel of the voice dreams
and so the depth is not just personal
words come to him
       heavy as stone
              sometimes fruitful
or sharp like fish bones
he sees a procession too

long ready to sing a requiem
        and laugh.
Why not
and one muscle cord in him
snaps with laughter
with the depth of dream
all that was black
        becomes clear and white
and the whiteness is a disastrous omen

this is why he is not against relief
through underground caves
        and new tunnels
through streets full of silts and mud
he sees in the distance a pebble
        that has swum out of death
starting to glow
        then turning
        and by turning deciding
                to be fruitful
it wishes to discover for itself
a new language

to be transparent as a glass marble
and instead of taking divine forms
        in itself excellent
to have somebody sublime
to be constantly faithful to him.

This newborn stone
was the apparition of a woman

who tied it round her waist
the tiger has visions
        of all-knowing tigerhood
for the peacock another conceited crown
for each of them their own
        apotheosis prepares within
still no-one says clearly
        I AM

I am the one that sings
        and brings food
bridges the world with love
before the least god
        remains without voice
and once more emerges
in the mockery that sticks out from somewhere
and removes denial as acuteness
worthy of a hero and monk

I am the only one who dares
        to recognize himself
and to stand up when it is required
        who is guilty
the miracle of the Lepenic whirlpool
pleader for the women and family
the point on which silence leans
and a reason loud and clear
        I AM

10.

And before the wedding is over
being the bride, I must roar out
to let him know that he marries thunder
and becomes one with the lightning
Once upon a time I was beautiful
above a grave
      in Mesopotamia
then the priest
      raised me on high
and over the arch of night
sent me to the north coasts
and here I stand now in brown radiance
on the walls of Gamzigrad
between exaggerated magic
      and inexhaustible fruit
incarnate in a new image
akin to Asian abandon
and I guard your vineyards
for the best sons and daughters
      of your kind.

But that is not all that induces
the authority of an ancient goddess
      between me and the sun
there is neither opposites nor war
let him just hold on to
his red-hot underworld
from which daily he takes out
      a nugget with a tail

I stay in the centre of great pain
with the sounds of red dark
and I sharpen the blade
that will lay bare the gifts
      of the dark bride
in the depths of the wood
where the women gather now
separated from brother, father and god
and lure into a reel all that is fertile
      seeds
prevents disease
and again she is detested
when the voice of the bridegroom echoes
high above the clouds and marble
detestably in the town square
      all those
that do not wish to see the measureless space of the night
which is neither for man nor prophet
but for an ancient ruler
destroyer of all that bows
to a new eminence.

So you married round the moon
and round the willow
we became accustomed to a double guarantee
and another cause always appears
the third
our customs are located
      in a Triplefaith
an ancient book tells of it too
there are three gates to our town

for the killer knights
for the priest
or man of science
and lastly for the many peasants
        and artisans
This is how weddings bind us
round the tree
        the heavenly body
               and round the book
leaning on the Triangle
we stand firmly
we hold together
lower and higher cares.

Never have we lived in the singular
neither have our solitaries
        in the forest
        the cave
        on the lake water
        languished without the trinity
and so in weddings
        two genders gather
or Three unite.

from *Sequence*

1.

Uphill
someone
walks
hopes for
a lighted
trail

at rest is
natural
ignorance

a butterfly
just
through the touch
of flowers
declares
something

a shadow
bars the way
from above
like a hand

the clouds
stand
at the top
where
the phase
began

before the entrance
into the shadow
a morning
membrane
remained

2.

Up
in the branches
a clap
of wings
a raven heads
north
he is offered
a sacrifice
over the ice

the day of rest
leaves its own trunks
aside
the trees
seek
tenderness
and bow
their head
to the centre

conifers
caress
in the cupola
the voice of
the pine cone
rings
on the stone
floor

the sun
holds
the poet's
robe
and the anonymity
of the grave

3.

Milk
is drunk
grass
drinks
juniper
intensifies
its wind
the sky
prepares
for storms
hawk-eyed

in the forest
the lighthouse
wanders
the trees
dance
the I-Ching
the clouds
through the change
a ring
of water
in the realm
of storm

lovely is
the weather
in a glass
of water

4.

Across the crag
goes
in a gown
white
or dreams
first
through the crowd
then
leads
to the place
of gathering
of its brother
in a spiral
a snail
bloodless
and holy
like water
air
flame
deaf
puts it down
for seeds
between
the creator
loud
and the destroyer
avid

did not

bestow
an oration
on the Mount
of Olives

5.

In the summer
grass
your hand
did not even
find itself

neither
did it create
the clouds
and passed
over
the rough
bark
that haunts
the oaks
and pines

now light
sounds
over the stems
and wishes
to return
all the uplands
to you

later
everybody
will be
created

in the palm of your hand
above the leap
of a doe
and in the dark
glade
in the skeleton
of the forest

6.

I will turn
the golden
glove
that holds you
inside out

from the fingers
gravel
rotten
bones
and temples
will tumble

made of
snow
is its other side
and the whiteness will
witness
in wonder
when the glove
begins
to pluck out
deceits
from the garden
of the body

To you
that
drew on

the left
glove
so that
my right hand
suffers

7.

Silence
its
verge
is stepped on

a butterfly
has lost
its face
in a flower

there is nobody
to see
the multiplicity
of its wings

the world
resembles
a living being

honey
has collected
at the bottom
of a tube

and worries
over winter
whether
tomorrow
petals

will utter
an eclogue

if the poem
beneath the earth
survives
the silence of the poet

8.

On a trail
hilly
limy
wait for me
a prophet
and herald
determined
to person-
ify
themselves
as a butterfly

Ezekiel
and Gabriel
heartily
agree
to minuteness

I watch them
as they fly
each
on one wing

to the One
that is omnipresent
this act
is a delight

And often
He dwindles
and passes
through his creatures
like an awl

10.

A walnut
walks
a trail
and a candle
follows
in its tracks

a tree
big
as a plane-tree
has grown
so a walnut
can be born

so a weevil
can burn
much
honeycomb
Is stacked up

and everybody has said
that life is
bitter
and that
hanging high
is the golden
burdock

a candle
walks
a trail
and a walnut
follows
in its tracks

11.

Leaves
bow
humbly
to someone
resist
the nettle
the poison ivy
the thorn-bush
and with them are
wasps
and bees

the reverse
of a general
order

worthy
of praise
at day-break
with hair
is everything
that
bites
scratches
burns
and all
with quills
poison
sword

but from the horned
only
the stag
is loved most

and only
from
the barbed
is ointment
best

13.

A snake
twists
when
it changes
direction
before
it
whirls
somebody away

This shape
wriggles
fast
as if
there are
two snakes
working
In the body

in the venomous
snake's
innards
another
snake
twists
quicker
than
the first

14.

Autumn
delays
its moment
earth's
surface
is a picture
green
brown
and lemon
colours
have covered
the mud

an epoch
of reduced
branches

from a horse
a horseman
becomes
nobody
returns
to the
first
nor does the woodsman
wish to transform
into his
tree

a woman
made
of locust
leaves
sits
at the foot
of the walker
then
lies down

her
image
stands up
soaring
and substantial
opposed
to our
shame

16.

A cloud
clouds
the sky
in a dirty
look
somebody now
sings
a song
to water
a big-eyed
shape
is drawn into
the dream
and the attic
the black
look
pleases
the dream
but the shape
pulls
and harrows
watches
like a father
and then
frowns
the son
has to
work
to plough

to prepare
furrows
for the rain
and for the one
that is
to be born
come
so
your forbear
can shape you
he says
and sends
thunder
to clout
you

xxx

Return, you saw the wing
close by the road. Who devours the birds
here and in the wind? Don't be
too strict, perhaps the wing
in the air consumes its body.
So fall and wait for somebody
to take possession of it: ant or the man
to whom that with the wing has already happened.

xxx

The creator, the great and true,
of necessity vanished, after completing
his creation.
        Something still turns.
a spirit, that copes with lawlessness
barely, and a son, in a world without mercy
dedicated to love, to which nothing compares
in weight, in dimension.

The Bacchae

A maternal sacrifice is made
in a sleepwalking ecstasy, a son is torn apart.
Dionysius arrives, deus ex machina,
to pronounce the sentence that says: exile;
for the obedient, and for those who were not this,
the same for all. Then thunder.
God has been the machine since the beginning,
that has moved all to the incestuous
crime. After the sin that he was driven to,
man remains alone at the verge of the abyss.
The thread of destiny is untied.
His will leads him, untrammeled,
and heedless.

22.

Lower
your head
to the ground
and touch it
with your hand
with the top of your head
and with your forehead

in it
break
your stick

in the middle
everything
is green
fresh
and rotten

at the back of the head
an airy
table
arises

of a new
division
of sky
and body
no-one has
heard

exactly

the sun
extends you
red
salt

23.

Man is
the measure
of all things
and like
a meter
doesn't know
its own
size
nor does a man
understand
how to measure
himself

once
he accepts
the vastness
and gives in
to faith
and the universe

the second time
he finds
trust
in Nothing
and compares himself
to naught

the third
time

with the length
of his shadow
he tries to
take
his own
measure

Which is how
a man
alone in the woods
yields himself
into the hands
of a beast darker
than himself

from *Second Sequence*

3.

Morning
noticed me
almost brisk
between the marigold
and the buttercup

Delight
before the world
and fear
of encountering
a woodsman
bloody-handed
and blue skinned

Horror
and ecstasy
look like
one another

Let
opposites
erase
each other

And you breathe

Don't shout

4.

A heap of ashes
on the path

flakes dark blue
white
greyblack

A winged radiance
is ready to burst
from the embers

On a live coal
wisdom
ripens

But whose?

Mine
mine
or mine

Ants
butterflies
roe deer bicker

Silent is he
who lit the fire
who raked together
a heap of ashes

6.

Those
who cleave to God
and want to be at one
with him

Likewise with those
who bow
to the flower

Their faith
lasts
only a summer

The prayer
then
goes to seed

9.

What dictates
the game
of subtraction?

Remove
the tree
so that you can see
the forest

Tear the leave
so that you can get
to the branch

Stop
breathing
to have
breath

Pull
the world
from its
image

Wanderers
of all sorts
beg you

from *Third Sequence*

This morning I saw
avid butterflies
on the balcony flowers

and their brown wings
over the bushes
where the ripe raspberry
nests

Into the meadow flowers
at the edge of woods
butterflies have planted themselves
and broadcast pollen

showing
that even those who can't see each other
can be in love

Mind

The mind is
an undecided
Perceiver

Which idea
to entertain?

With the uncreated
from where
its origins are

Or its history
in which everybody gets
a smoke

In the first case
it doesn't know how

In the second
it doesn't know
with whom

xxx

When he releases his bow
the archer looks long
as his arrow
wanders into the dark

The archer
is abandoned
to the pity and pitilessness
of his target

from *The Wise and Foolish Virgins*

There is a maiden-painting, too
ready for eternity with us
which the painter cannot find
nor the fisherman fetch from the sea
the purity
that nurses nobody
nor has the purpose of giving birth to gods
does not ascend to us from the great mother
nor from those women
that sat in a saddle
to make war against the male portion.
Her passion does not loot
nor does her wisdom enslave.
She is not an incarnation
neither of tribal nobility nor idea.
When the dawn breaks
she stands above the poplars
and spins a light fabric.
She takes you to far shores
from where bliss falls in abundance
over which the stars soar
To enter one part of her image
she turns to the one
she does not wish to disregard.
The girl of the morning
gazes gently and embraces indirectly
with hands of air
with the light spider web that flows
over the base of a sunbeam.
In her hand a glass rings
and the seas glitter

with her midnight too becomes light
passes through the solemn gathering
as though instead of bones
she carries crystal
then goes straight to the mountain
in a long robe.
She watches the edges of the planet
and the far distances that glow
side by side with the sky.
She extends her palms and her brow.
She utters her name
in which a multitude crosses
sacrifice and knowledge
of love that opens all
so there is nothing any more
neither door frame nor door nor sun
on the top of the temple.
She alone remains united
with the maidenhood
that goes high
above the Milky Way
though the movement is of the same direction
as the murmuring in the breast
which breathes
and proves that she is not a statue.
Behold words emerge from beneath lace
and foam over the glass
where there is an inexhaustible well.
In the midst of love she offers meaning
and stands above it
as over a forest

wide-eyed and of smooth image.
She has managed to affect all
while you take pride in her image.
She is above nature
like a cupola.
Beneath her human bodies
have lacerated each other in torment
like forty martyrs
emerging from the ice.
All gain new clothes
and propose a toast to her
who helped to bear burdens
long and painfully
and then to be cast aside
down under a bloody peak.
For the old world they neither shed a tear nor let it go.
They forget how their mother was
And what thought pursues
riding on one's skull
as though it were a car.
She offers light in abundance

So the maiden may live
she reveals herself in the mind!

The Lovers in the Church

If Laza Kostić had not versified
Santa Maria della Salute
on the other side of the Grand Canal
somebody would have written a poem about the painting
of Saint Barbara in the church.
of Santa Maria Formosa

She combines youth and ripeness,
victorious with a palm branch and a wheel
torture instead of a halo: the torments
that precede salvation, or are
consequent on the reasons for salvation.

Bodies shudder, an omen
of passion, and the lovers pray
for passion to remain, before an image
which will not bring a poem:
accomplished beauty becomes Revelation.

Bacchus and Ariadne in Naxos

Baccho has got on top of the car like Harlequin
and is waving the king's cape, Ariadne
comes out of the bedroom in grey
and red. The beginning of a wedding or invitation
to a licentious progress? Two moves
in a contrary game: heavenly gentlemen

have special theatrical privileges:
Dionysius much too young for the part,
She to see something sizeable in the marriage
Between them, the island coast's luxuriance.
And a blue abyss where that
which is terrible becomes beautiful.

Entering Cremona I

Above the sanctity the Inteletto d'amore
is discovered again, like a jewel
That is kept quiet in half-shadow
The hymn's gravity has replaced debauchery.
A goddess that bodes ill, acquiesces in
the rejuvenation of her own image

and the encounters of lovers in the square
in front of the cathedral. The girl has
overpowered the guards, so who's the victim now?
Perugino has elevated beauty
to judge him severely, to be

beyond remorse, and above the people.

Giorgione: La Tempesta

Separation begins when maturity passes.
Everybody stands on his own side of the river.
The town is not just closed, it exists less.
Exile is more necessary than courage.
Even the bridge no longer joins, nor spans the river;
Metaphor moves away from the century.

The husband dressed, the woman in an unpleasing
    nakedness
He is the guard by the grave, she feeds the coming
    generation;
as though a cloud will drench the earth
and the brook in spate will counterattack.
Lightning sends a message to the picture: humanity's space
is shrinking. He steps aside, and towards the West.

Exile from Paradise, The Flight to Egypt,
A scene from the life of Adam and Eve?
Without title this discharge remains.
A smell of sulphur in a green shudder.
One stands before the storm without any true conscience;
in this lies the separation, the parting, the skysplit

Visiting the Zoological Gardens in Winter

The paths are snowbound
and dusk falls early.
the bench is striped white
like a zebra, under it
a dark rabbit hunched tight
and two peacocks by the closed kiosk
are looking for crumbs.
The sky has bent from its grey
burden. Since I was here
last and now after visiting
the hospital I go to a little piece
of childhood and seek evidence
of remaining strength and wildness.

You knock at the gate politely
then you see two young giraffes
in a dark corner, a little flame smoulders.
On the right two elephants stand idly
like docked ships. Outside
a fallow deer kicks out his legs
slim and still ready for wide open spaces.
Bison stand under the snow;
immobile roofs of straw
Their gaze cannot catch
anybody, it looks aside too much.
Small pheasants glide, it's time
to tangle their family confusions.
Parrots in another pavilion
squawk, drenched in red and muddy gold,
as though they slaughtered one another.

I listen long, truly an invitation
to yell and shriek
and let your voice go free. Between the cages
and the jungle balances are certain.
Nobody sleeps more quietly than the python,
the anaconda immersed in its own poison.
Peace in the garden: no different are
the boa constrictor and the worm.

On the brink of the muddy water eagerly
expecting its feeder
the hippopotamus, like a believer listens to
the sound of Easter bells.
The alligator clings to the shallow bottom,
As though having an attack of paralysis.
I pass by the apes
who live multi-storey.
A rabbit runs across the snow
like a shoe that walks alone.
Just the panther is ready for anything,
for winter, heat and hunger,
and in a small space succeeds
to wander, hunt, knock things over and cast a spell;
a knight in a greenish dolmen
and a barefoot exile.

A deer horns the Chinese grate
or cut into thin rings, and eat
for strength and renewal, thus
one could begin to use a camel hump and bison's beard,
a peacock's tail, a tiger's hair, and what an eagle

wears round its neck. Perhaps this could help
the sick woman who has lain for two months
and losing speech. When I saw her
behind the broken doors, she seemed already dead.
Eyes open, she had half-slipped from
the bed already. Incontinent. Then she
started speaking like Eleazar. Cold-blooded
frailty. And the spectacle of a soul becoming numb.
    Damned
November, such that no kind of hoping,
nor an opening from the other side, can oppose.

It's as if a sin is gloating, one that cancels
childhood, Christmas, and a maternal
overheated idol. After the third stroke
nobody can correct the circuits
of the brain. Metaphysical thought had been
shattered by a stroke, I watch the hips of a zebra,
monkeys that delay in expectation,
a she panther almost green from fury,
in a quarrel with lumps of ice, an alligator
mandala, and the last pharaoh – the Nile horse.
All have freely given up the right to speak,
and the family novel. Is this not –
where redemption is? The Zoological gardens are better
than a pharmacy. After a visit to the hospital
It shows itself as a guarantee of continuing
and wild life, and as a treasury of health.

Emmanuel De Witt: A Girl at the Virginals

Was it before or after midday that found
the girl inclined above the virginal?
The illuminated pavements look like notes.
The image is divided into three rooms
like music in three movements. The painter
is represented as what is played.

Or the musician took into her hands
what the painting wanted to evoke.
The notes are light and shadow.
Every object is pure acoustic:
glass, dresser board, curtain
velvet and the window ... itself is a miracle,

Its light surpasses the wisdom
of the century. That wisdom changed to music,
has been decided by this space.
Irrevocable. Its waves fall back
from the wallpaper; the hardness of reality
has achieved itself. And opens no longer.

A Flemish Painter

Who has the right
       to be in a painting?
Once
only God
       and his retinue
then the emperor
       and his court
the head of the church
and the greatest heroes
       then the duke
and merchants with a bag
       in their hand
Oh I'm fed up with that
even ragamuffins
look refined
when they're eating melon
formally fluttering
       their tears
       and tatters
I want to paint
       everyday things
       from the kitchen
the dead jug
       the scanty pot lid
and a blanched chicken
bread on a board
humble ants
and faces on a crust,
that expect and endure
       everything from us,
shaggy asparagus

            sausages
            as if of resin
and the healthy bodies of onions
all at the keen summit
            of simple hunger,
            mine
or whoever's,
their simple being
turning to my brush
            that honours them
Yet the picture itself
            is much too good
            Oh misery,
this pot of beer
costs
as if it were gold
and the shadow of vegetables
exceeds in price
the most expensive markets,
            for art there is
            no threshold low enough
and poverty is expensive
            and a fly
for the one who wishes
to keep them in a picture!

Imaginary Journey

23rd October, a Sunday,
a day of not going to India,
the time when I was supposed to sit
at the airport and wait, gloomy,
a Sunday departure, in the many
being alone. In a mist of silence
where Agra shows itself
a dead man at the wheel on the road
to the Taj Mahal, and a herd of cheerful monkeys
and the muddy Ganges, soiled
where human ashes are laundered
and a yogi waits for the sun to rise
at an inside gate where no-one
raises a wall any more. Even the dawn
doesn't have a sign except the noise
opposite a plain similar to Banat
and gold-plated cupolas, and under these
no god, known to me, resides.

Remain unseen Bhubaneshvar in Orissa,
Konarak and the temples in Pura,
Khajuraho awakes mysterious
and borne away to the wedding of the moon
in stages and climbing a ladder
in the skies on whose power this sunset
depends. The day of not coming is a flicker
in Lingham in the depth of Kandariya-
Mahadev and Kailasanatha and on the face
of the higher Vishnu. They think of me
the stone shells of Pattadakal, of Madurai
and a snake stretched from Gwalior to Badami.

In Mahabalipuram a god
goes blind while staring at the sea
and the lustful duke Chadela
prays to the goddess Durga to even out
his passions for love and war.

You do not have to breathe in everything, nor touch,
distance is a kind of respect,
and mercy is required to conquer her,
compassion contrary to the algebra of a love knot.
The thought follows the blue bird,
from behind the Jain building;
Mahavira finds that sanctuary cramped
and he would like to fly wherever a branch
dropped from the sky calls him. The indecent crucifixion
has managed to attract the gods
if the victory is to be a redeeming darkness
which accepts the unfulfilled
souls of passengers, on the crossroads
of the stellar navel, in the depths
of the invisible temple.

from *The Danube Valley*

From above the Wild Rock and its fort
into the abyss a witness gazes with the one-shouldered sun,
And sees the river winding, from Paradise
Just emerging, a crystal device of flowing.
Michael floats over it, he protects from Hell,
those who were expelled for no true reason
and struggle in couples around the field between sharp cliffs

The founders of cultivation where everything is different
From the manners of the highlands where it all began.
It was not worth tasting knowledge from the tree
Because exile has changed the truths.
Knowledge is a purely physical matter here.
Outside paradise light has become shorter
but the creatures have multiplied.

I watch the green Danube flow away
The source of the church bells that I hear
From the depths as Moma used to hear
The word that moves all, from the beginning.
Shankara breathed the same as the most virtuous of monks
From Hilandar, let's say Teodosije:
Thought is the base of breath. Then one and another
open the doors in being and carry its idea.
All of this was written down on a grand of pages
and became part of the liturgy served
in the pedestal of the Mother of God.
Every part of the body wants to surrender to this work
and make a song of the heights around the high dome.

from *Orgia Sacra*

10.

Above the doorway a lion
sticks out his tongue
and its flames are
beginning of the temple
since the temple once was
a dragon, too,
and when it reached
two metres in height
the stone-mason locked the tongue
into the winding form
of a grape-bearing stem
from which bunches
grow out sideways,
thus the stone
is part of the wine
that is granted at the dining table
as a sign of honours
to the altar,
with a thick bunch of grapes
you can give communion
to every rogue
that squats
on the top of the portal
joyful that even over him
a head sprouts
and shines through while it climbs
flower by flower
towards the one and only sky
that it makes fruitful.

The End of the Orgy

The orgy ends when it approaches a wedding
or the moon sets behind the hill and the bacchants
one by one are broken over their knees
Fall over the burning sheaves. It seems
as if a world just created has shown its weary sinking,
in other words being has stopped striking its rhythm;
dust has remained on the path and in the place of the stake
or the phoenix left its ashes on the doorstep
(the news arrived today that La Feniche has burned,
who knows what times are these that an opera house disappears
    in flames)
but you can hear about the new assault of the magic crane
from the region of the Yin and Yang, and the firebird shows itself
on the coasts of the ice sea and here at the black mountain,
in the cave of the dragon underground magnets are attempting
to make a soul fly down to each embryo.
The Dragon-man remains worthy of his ritual
(a slippery cave of good report, the best along with the one
that gives many gold zlotys) and the best insight
and true state of affairs has the anciently known Snake Reel –
there next to the ogre the head of a medusa grins
which means: an open snake mouth seizing tails
on return from a journey round the Earth's pattern
a trip that is achieved by trembling through snake
tails (or: body) similar to the circuit through which a current flows
alternately male and female strength – never
held in it is every whelp conceived
and every dead man swaddled and this is the flame
fanned by our instincts; the orgy might stop
but the snake's **rut** never ceases
We don't know from where his geometric image came

which gives birth to the wave and the spouting of the geyser
but the creative circle is coiled around the entire universe
visible to the naked eye and the body of the equinox
which shares its supremacy with itself
thus with the spirit that has many synonyms
and endures through them every day saying: farewell!

from *The Science of the Soul*

xxx

In parentheses and at the end: the ways of the soul are chancy.
One doesn't know to where it might stray, fall by the wayside:
on a dusty shelf, in a neglected chimney,
on an island that knows no prayer,
into card files whose entries about it are spiteful.
Some even wish to separate from it
saying that it's evil, lustful and incoherent.
But there again, who take upon themselves any vow?
Other than the one that the I has promised to itself!
Or to accept what the travel guide whispers
while uniting with us, – that we are required to be
absolutely metaphysical !?

Note

This choice of poems was made by the author himself. The poems are arranged according to the years of publication, concluding with the newest that were not previously published elsewhere. The poems originate from the period of 50 years, from 1946 to 1996, and were chosen into this book on the basis of their similarity. Their starting point is the concreteness of the sensory perceptions, erotic inspiration and experiencing scenes from nature.

www.ingramcontent.com/pod-product-compliance
Lightning Source LLC
Chambersburg PA
CBHW031136090426
42738CB00008B/1111